About The Author:

Elliot Emerson is a partner and part-time university student. With their first book reaching number 16 in 'Psychology & Mental Health: Hot New releases' in the first approximately 48 hours of release. This was a huge achievement to Elliot, as someone who has expressed throughout their work, writing was never to be imagined, only a few months ago. Music really influences the way that Elliot formulates starting points in each chapter, as well as taking outer influences from friends, family and other authors.

Elliot expresses openly that they have a form of Post-Traumatic Stress Disorder, through their upbringing. Elliot always knew that there was more than low level anxiety.

Elliot has found writing to a form of artistic therapy, the thing they have been trying to find. Elliot wouldn't have done any of this if it weren't for their partner and a good friend, who recently started their author journey. They hope you find comfort in this book, and future work. Elliot states they would like to "create a sense of family" something they have been missing throughout their childhood.

Elliot hopes you'll enjoy the ride and remember, put your mental health and recovery first… oh and do not ever apologies for being who you are!

Pre-Chapter: Hello, again!

Hello, if you're reading this then I hope it's out of learning and understanding, o
to metaphorically say curiosity killed the cat.

Unfortunately, I have a feeling that isn't the case. I'd like to say you won't
resonate with any of this book, but if you do. I'm sorry!

I'm sorry life wasn't kind to you, please reach out for support and this comes
with a huge TRIGGER WARNING! This contains mental health and abuse
themes throughout, including rejection, domestic abuse and more. Please DO
NOT read this novel if it is detrimental to your mental health. Your safety is
much more important to me than you reading my words.

Again, stay safe, and I'm sorry,
Elliot.

Chapter 1: Starting with My Father

I'm going to start with my father... the only parent I still speak to. The relationship that puts me on edge. The way we fight, my instinct is to walk away but my rejection issues make me stay. Can I live without both my mom and my dad?

And then…

We will move onto my so-called Mom!

Chapter 2: The Only Parent I Still Speak To.

The only parent I still speak to, you shout at everyone so loud.

The only parent I still speak to, you come across so cold, you blame it on becoming *old*.

The only parent I still speak to, I wish you would acknowledge you could have done more!

If only I took videos of me crying on the bathroom floor.

The only parent I still speak to, as my Dad I wish you did more.

Chapter 3: Again Dad

Dear Dad,

You said it again,

And again,

And again.

She's manipulative,

So why did you let her manipulate my head!

Chapter 4: Dad, You Did This!

Dad, you did this,

Look what you have done,

I thought with me, her battle was won,

Now she is doing it to your other child,

Now you are fuming, what got you mad.

Surely, you knew this was to come,

She doesn't want us, and then the battle will be won.

I thought she wouldn't be like this, after she lost your only son!

Chapter 5: Dad, Is This a Picture?

Oh Daddy...

I was only a child,

The only child at the time,

Is it true?

Or is it a nightmare?

I have this picture, sitting in my mind,

Does not matter how many times I ask, Daddy...

It really will not leave, the picture I saw.

Is it true? Did you pin my mother up the wall?

Chapter 6: The Sirens Are at The Door!

Nee-Naw, Nee-Naw...

The sirens are at the door,

Daddy, is it you they are looking for?

Oh Daddy, did she do it again?

Oh God, no!

The b*tch has done it again...

She's called the police to have you removed again!

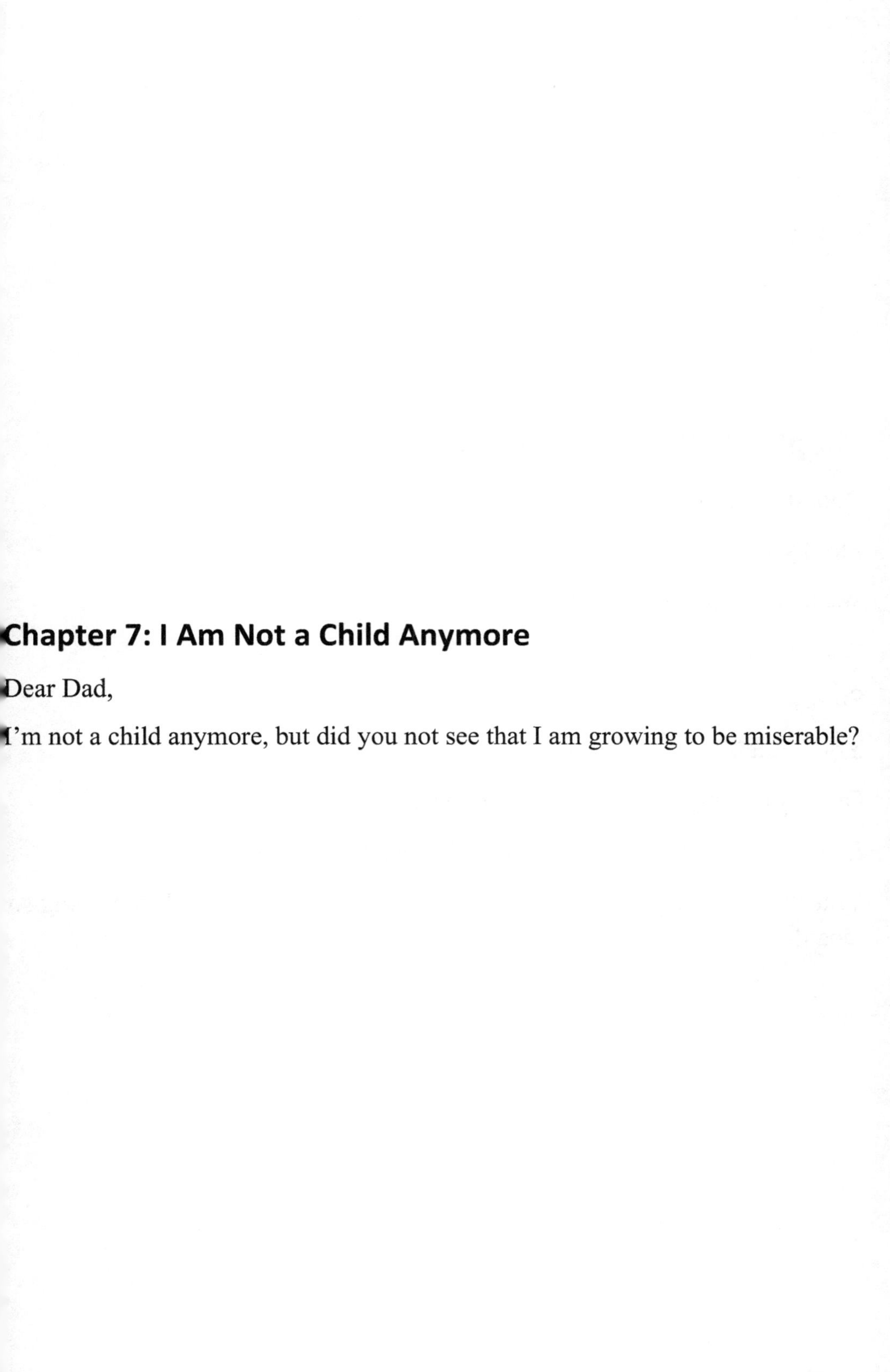

Chapter 7: I Am Not a Child Anymore

Dear Dad,

I'm not a child anymore, but did you not see that I am growing to be miserable?

Chapter 8: Dad, It's Me Again

Dad, it's me again...

I told you to get out my life again,

We had another argument,

It's time to take a bow...

Surely if you loved me,

You wouldn't say the things.

Only you thought was appropriate to say.

Even now I'm in my twenties, and this happened in my teens,

You still revert to the same kinds of words, I wish you would stop being so mean!

Chapter 9: Truth

It's time to tell the truth Dad.

It was only the other day, you were screaming,

You spoke about the things you *attempted* to protect her from,

The pictures, the boys, the internet...

If only you knew, I ended up in similar positions too.

See... the thing is, you created that bond with your other child,

She became Daddy's little princess if you will, you spoilt her...

Or did she manipulate you?

Why did you presume... just because I was quiet, that I was okay?

Surely as a parent, so little noise can be scary?

Chapter 10: Will You Ever Stop the Drinking Dad?

Will you ever stop the drinking Dad?

I honestly do not know if your health will last.

You have a temper, just admit it please Dad.

You made me out to be the bad guy, but I was worried at last.

Oh, go on, please Dad.

Dad please, the cans got darker, and stronger…

Will you please remember what happened to your dad?

Will you ever stop the drinking Dad?

You are getting better Dad; it isn't as bad.

It's mainly on weekends but Dad, even now I'm an adult, you are still getting mad!

As teenager, you flipped it, blamed it all on me!

The atmosphere got so loud; my nan called the police!

I, the teenager in the back of the car; you had my sister, just please safely get her back.

Dad, I am an adult now; I drink occasionally too.

My parents are alcoholics, but I can leave the drink unlike the pair of you!

Oh god, please Dad be careful.

I believe, you should quit the drinking, will you ever stop though Dad?

Chapter 11: Oh "Mom", I Don't Know...

Oh "Mom", I don't know where to start, I struggling even call you my mother now.

Oh "Mom", why are you so mad? I don't know what I ever did,

Oh "Mom", please tell me now!

I sit here and wonder, I sit in and sob, oh mother please tell me what I have done!

Oh "Mom", most of the pain is recent, most of the pain is new, it really isn't though mum.

Oh "Mom" please tell the truth!

How did you do it?

How did you hide it, all the abuse?

Oh "Mom", stop using my name as an excuse for the abuse!

Chapter 12: You Aren't What I Dreamed Of?

You aren't what I dreamed of; I think it was a mistake.

You weren't the mother I dreamt of, in the daytime nor at night.

I needed someone who was caring, who would always put me first!

Oh dear, mother! You have really made it worse!

Now as an adult, I'm broken and occasionally insecure!

You aren't what I dreamed of, I think it was a mistake; I thought I was your baby, your eldest… but did you ever mean your "I love you(s)", or was I your mistake?

Chapter 13: Why Mom? Why?

Mom, oh please, just tell me why?

Why my heart hurts on the inside?

My insides sit and knot in fear, of what you'll call me next my dear.

I do not understand, you have nothing on me,

Is that it? You can no longer control me?

Mom, oh please, just tell me why?

Why did you treat me the way you did?

Missed my important life events, like you did.

Pushed me physically, mentally and emotionally,

You did it all.

Yet the days, I hit by lowest, I still question why.

Because sometimes amongst it all, I need my mom sometimes!

So, mother just please tell me why; why do you keep doing this to me!

Chapter 14: Mom, Is It True?

Mom…

Mom…

Mom… is it true?

Is it you that is in hospital?

Mom…

Mom…

Mom… is it true?

Is it you that made them black and blue?

Mom…

Mom…

Mom… is it true?

Is it you that you tried to die?

Mom…

Mom…

Mom… is it true?

Is it true that nobody can get it through to you?

Mom…

Mom…

Mom… I really don't know what anyone can say to you!

Chapter 15: Social Media

Your life is a soap opera, on repeat at all times.

You record, snap it and put it free online.

You made the headlines; the platforms mentioned your name!

You tell everyone your business; you complain when the episodes repeat again and again!

You were part of the gossip, part of spreading the drama.

You attempted time and time again to try again.

You can't delete the evidence, delete the past.

If you don't want us to know your business…

Just stop allowing people to ask.

Your children aren't allowed to tell your business; isn't that what you said?

So why is it on Facebook; you've created a soap opera again!

Chapter 16: Do You Remember That Neighbour?

Mom…

Mom…

Mom… can I ask you a question?

Do you remember that neighbour?

No, not that one; don't be daft!

The house we lived in; the one you shared with dad?

Mom…

Mom…

Mom… can I ask you question?

Do you remember that neighbour?

No, not that neighbour; stop having a laugh!

The house with the woman that now reminds me of you!

Mom…

Mom…

Mom… can I ask you question?

Do you remember that neighbour?

Yes, that's the one; she set her house on fire!

She worried us all; she nearly destroyed the family neighbourhood!

Mom…

Mom…

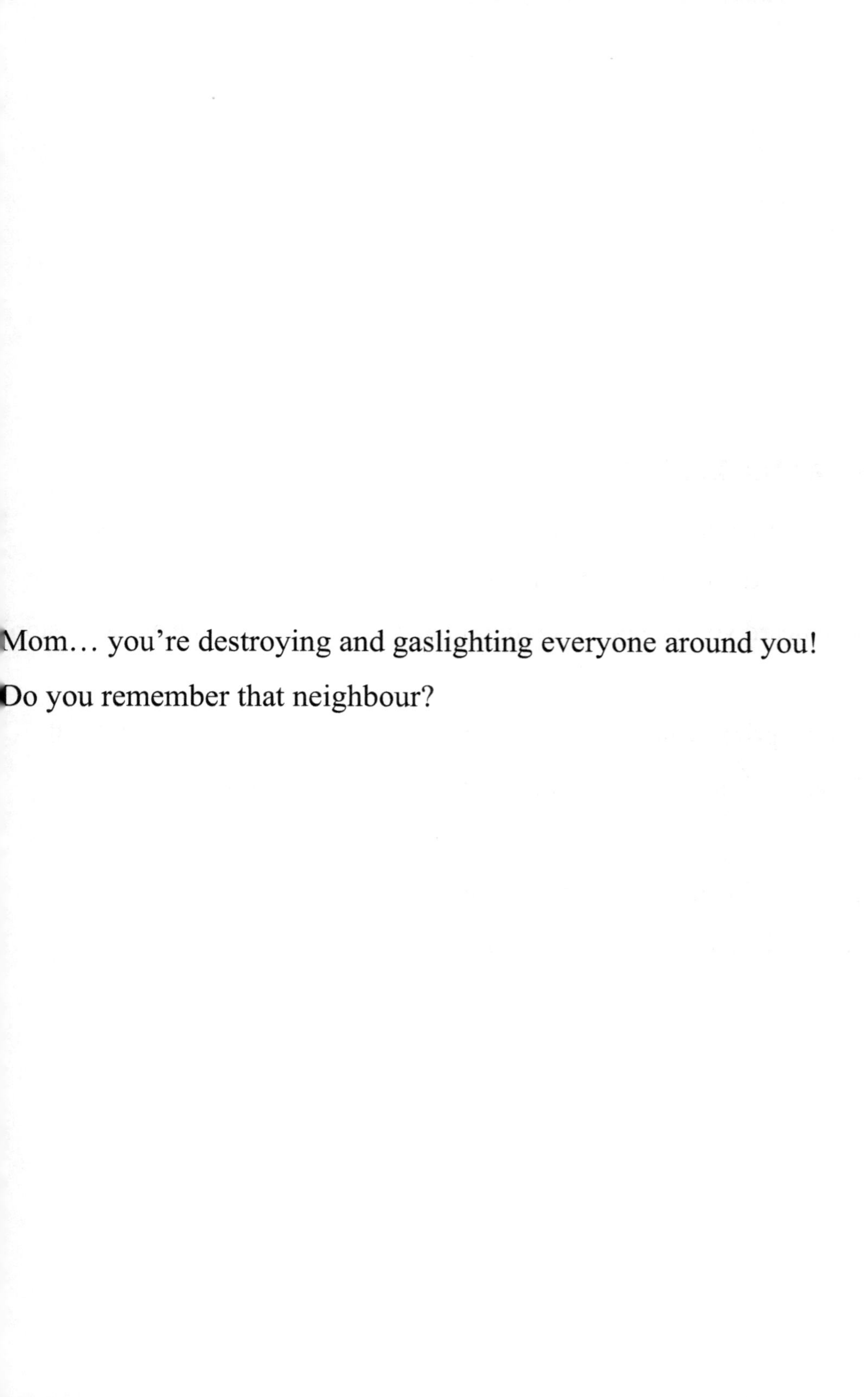
Mom… you're destroying and gaslighting everyone around you!
Do you remember that neighbour?

Chapter 17: I've Heard…

I've heard you've been drinking; I have heard you've lost control.

I've heard you seem out of it most days.

I've heard you've been drinking; I have heard you've been asked to stop!

I'm surprised you are still going; yes, I am surprised you aren't dead!

Please… if not for you; do it for your children for goodness's sake!

I've heard you've drinking; I've heard it's got dangerous.

Just look at what it did for my dad's dad!

Chapter 18: Dear Parents, Why Me?

Dear Parents, after all I ever did for you.

After all the complications; I shouldn't be alive!

All the times you failed me; I look back… did you ever care?

Dear Parents, before I hit my twenties, I found a way to be free!

I still stuck around to support you; cause remember you always needed me!

We all suffer with trauma; I get that I do!

However, I have a couple things to ask…

Did it give you the right to do the things you did?

Or allow other people to f*ck their kid up too?

One final question, my mother and my father.

Dear Parents, Why Me?

My Complicated Recovery Series:

I hope you enjoyed the second book in the series!

If you haven't already check out *"Apparently, I'm Complicated: Version 2"*, now available in paperback! Scan the QR to check it out!

What's Next In 2021?

We are three quarters of the way into 2021… I know I cannot believe it too!

Here is a sneak peak into my next trauma-based book, The Pain and The Void.

I'll share an extract:

Chapter 1: The Void, How Did You Destroy Me?

My soul wasn't enough, I am not the only soul you are trying to take! Your children feel like dying for goodness' sake! Is there a reason some of us were born with chances of not surviving or didn't quite make it? You believe in signs, I know that! It was a sign that you couldn't keep these innocent beings safe! They were too special for you and yet I made it, I was the first! Did the spirits see the way you were treating me?

www.ingramcontent.com/pod-product-compliance
Lightning Source LLC
Chambersburg PA
CBHW072347270726
48659CB00023B/2433